Date: ——/——/——

"Trust because y...

risk, not because it's safe or certain." --

Anonymous

Date: ——/——/——

"It always seems impossible until it's done."

-- Nelson Mandela

Date: ——/——/——

"If you want to achieve greatness stop asking for permission." --Anonymous

----

Date: ____/____/____

"Things work out best for those who make the best of how things work out." --John Wooden

----

Date: ——/——/——

"To live a creative life, we must lose our fear of being wrong." --Anonymous

----

Date: ——/——/——

"If you are not willing to risk the usual you will have to settle for the ordinary." --Jim Rohn

----

Date: ——/——/——

"Success is walking from failure to failure with no loss of enthusiasm." Winston Churchill

---

Date: ——/——/——

"Blessed are those who can give without remembering and take without forgetting." --
Anonymous

Date: ——/——/——

"Do one thing every day that scares you." --
Anonymous

Date: ——/——/——

"What's the point of being alive if you don't at least try to do something remarkable." -- Anonymous "

Date: ___/___/___

"Life is not about finding yourself. Life is about creating yourself." --Lolly Daskal

----

Date: ——/——/——

"Nothing in the world is more common than unsuccessful people with talent." --Anonymous

----

Date: ——/——/——

"Knowledge is being aware of what you can do. Wisdom is knowing when not to do it." -- Anonymous

----

Date: ——/——/——

"Your problem isn't the problem. Your reaction is the problem." --Anonymous

----

Date: ——/——/——

"You can do anything, but not everything." –
Anonymous

Date: ——/——/——

"Innovation distinguishes between a leader and a follower." *--Steve Jobs*

Date: ____/____/____

"Champion is afraid of losing. Everyone else is afraid of winning." – Billie Jean King

----

Date: ——/——/——

"Thinking should become your capital asset, no matter whatever ups and downs you come across in your life." --A.P.J. Abdul Kalam

----

Date: ——/——/——

"I find that the harder I work, the more luck I seem to have." -- Thomas Jefferson

----

Date: ——/——/——

"The starting point of all achievement is desire."
-- Napoleon Hill

Date: ——/——/——

"Success is the sum of small efforts, repeated day-in and day-out." -- *Robert Collier*

Date: ——/——/——

"If you want to achieve excellence, you can get there today. As of this second, quit doing less-than-excellent work." -- Thomas J. Watson

---

Date: ——/——/——

"All progress takes place outside the comfort zone." --Michael John Bobak

----

Date: ——/——/——

"You may only succeed if you desire succeeding; you may only fail if you do not mind failing." -- *Philippos*

Date: ——/——/——

"Courage is resistance to fear, mastery of fear-- not absence of fear." --Mark Twain

----

Date: ——/——/——

"Only put off until tomorrow what you are willing to die having left undone."

-- Pablo Picasso

Date: ——/——/——

"People often say that motivation doesn't last. Well, neither does bathing--that's why we recommend it daily." --Zig Ziglar

----

Date: ____/____/____

"We become what we think about most of the time, and that's the strangest secret."

--Earl Nightingale

Date: ——/——/——

"The only place where success comes before work is in the dictionary." -- Vidal Sassoon

---

Date: ——/——/——

"Too many of us are not living our dreams because we are living our fears." --Les Brown

----

Date: ——/——/——

"I find that when you have a real interest in life and a curious life, that sleep is not the most important thing." --Martha Stewart

---

Date: ——/——/——

"It's not what you look at that matters, it's what you see." --Anonymous

----

Date: ——/——/——

"The road to success and the road to failure are almost exactly the same." *-- Colin R. Davis*

Date: ——/——/——

*"Success is liking yourself, liking what you do,
and liking how you do it."* --*Maya Angelou*

Date: ——/——/——

"As we look ahead into the next century, leaders will be those who empower others." -- Bill Gates

Date: ——/——/——

"A real entrepreneur is somebody who has no safety net underneath them." --Henry Kravis

---

Date: ——/——/——

"The first step toward success is taken when you refuse to be a captive of the environment in which you first find yourself." --Mark Caine

----

Date: ——/——/——

"Losers quit when they fail. Winners fail until they succeed." –Robert T. Kiyosaki

----

Date: ——/——/——

"When I dare to be powerful, to use my strength in the service of my vision, then it becomes less and less important whether I am afraid." --Audre Lorde

----

Date: ——/——/——

"Whenever you find yourself on the side of the majority, it is time to pause and reflect." -- Mark Twain

----

Date: ——/——/——

"There is no traffic jam along the extra mile."

--Roger Staubach

Date: ——/——/——

"Develop success from failures. Discouragement and failure are two of the surest stepping stones to success." --Dale Carnegie

----

Date: ——/——/——

"If you don't design your own life plan, chances are you'll fall into someone else's plan. And guess what they have planned for you? Not much." --Jim Rohn

----

Date: ____/____/____

"If you genuinely want something, don't wait for it--teach yourself to be impatient." --Gurbaksh Chahal

----

"Don't let the fear of losing be greater than the excitement of winning." -- Robert Kiyosaki

----

Date: ——/——/——

"If you want to make a permanent change, stop focusing on the size of your problems and start focusing on the size of you!" -- T. Harv Eker

---

Date: ——/——/——

"Life is what happens to you while you're busy making other plans." John Lennon

----

Date: ——/——/——

"Two roads diverged in a wood and I took the one less traveled by, and that made all the difference." --Robert Frost

----

Date: ——/——/——

"The number one reason people fail in life is because they listen to their friends, family, and neighbors." --Napoleon Hill

----

Date: ——/——/——

"The secret of your future is hidden in your daily routine." – Mike Murdock

----

Date: ____/____/____

"In my experience, there is only one motivation, and that is desire. No reasons or principle contain it or stand against it." --Jane Smiley

---

Date: ——/——/——

"Success does not consist in never making mistakes but in never making the same one a second time." --George Bernard Shaw

----

Date: ——/——/——

"I don't want to get to the end of my life and find
that I lived just the length of it. I want to have
lived the width of it as well." -- Diane Ackerman

Date: ____/____/____

"You must expect great things of yourself before you can do them." --Michael Jordan

----

Date: ——/——/——

"Motivation is what gets you started. Habit is what keeps you going." --Jim Ryun

----

Date: ——/——/——

"People rarely succeed unless they have fun in what they are doing." -- Dale Carnegie

----

Date: ——/——/——

"*"There is no chance, no destiny, no fate, that can hinder or control the firm resolve of a determined soul." --Ella Wheeler Wilcox*

Date: ——/——/——

"Our greatest fear should not be of failure but of succeeding at things in life that don't really matter." -- Francis Chan

----

Date: ——/——/——

"You've got to get up every morning with determination if you're going to go to bed with satisfaction." --George Lorimer

----

Date: ——/——/——

"A goal is not always meant to be reached; it often serves simply as something to aim at." -
- Bruce Lee

Date: ——/——/——

"Success is ... knowing your purpose in life, growing to reach your maximum potential, and sowing seeds that benefit others." --John C. Maxwell

----

Date: ——/——/——

"Be miserable. Or motivate yourself. Whatever has to be done, it's always your choice." --
Wayne Dyer

Date: ——/——/——

"To accomplish great things, we must not only act, but also dream, not only plan, but also believe." --Anatole France

Date: ____/____/____

"Most of the important things in the world have been accomplished by people who have kept on trying when there seemed to be no help at all." -- *Dale Carnegie*

Date: ——/——/——

"You measure the size of the accomplishment by the obstacles you had to overcome to reach your goals." --Booker T. Washington

----

Date: ——/——/——

"Real difficulties can be overcome; it is only the imaginary ones that are unconquerable." -- Theodore N. Vail

---

Date: ——/——/——

"It is better to fail in originality than to succeed in imitation." --Herman Melville

----

Date: —— / —— / ——

"What would you do if you weren't afraid."

--Spencer Johnson

Date: ——/——/——

"Little minds are tamed and subdued by misfortune; but great minds rise above it." --
Washington Irving

Date: ____/____/____

"Failure is the condiment that gives success its flavor." -- Truman Capote

----

Date: ——/——/——

"Don't let what you cannot do interfere with what you can do." --John R. Wooden

---

Date: ——/——/——

"You may have to fight a battle more than once
to win it." --Margaret Thatcher

Date: ——/——/——

"When I win and when I lose, I take ownership of it, because I really am in charge of what I do."

-- Nicki Minaj

Date: ——/——/——

"The way to get started is to quit talking and begin doing." Walt Disney

----

Date: ——/——/——

"The question I ask myself almost every day is, 'Am I doing the most important thing I could be doing?'" Mark Zuckerberg

----

Date: ——/——/——

"I attribute my success to this: I never gave or took any excuse." -- *Florence Nightingale*

Date: ——/——/——

Date: ――/――/――

"The most common way people give up their power is by thinking they don't have any." --
Alice Walker

Date: ——/——/——

"All our dreams can come true if we have the courage to pursue them." -- *Walt Disney*

Date: ____/____/____

"The only way to do great work is to love what you do." Steve Jobs

----

Date: ——/——/——

"If you do what you always did, you will get what you always got." --Anonymous

---

Date: ——/——/——

"Success is walking from failure to failure with no loss of enthusiasm." -- Winston Churchill

----

Date: ——/——/——

"Just when the caterpillar thought the world was ending, he turned into a butterfly." -- Proverb

----

Date: ——/——/——

"Successful entrepreneurs are givers and not takers of positive energy." --Anonymous

Date: ——/——/——

"Whenever you see a successful person, you only see the public glories, never the private sacrifices to reach them." -- Vaibhav Shah

----

Date: ——/——/——

"Opportunities don't happen, you create them."

-- Chris Grosser

Date: ——/——/——

"Try not to become a person of success, but rather try to become a person of value." -- Albert Einstein

Date: ——/——/——

"Great minds discuss ideas; average minds discuss events; small minds discuss people." --Eleanor Roosevelt

----

Date: ——/——/——

"I have not failed. I've just found 10,000 ways that won't work." -- *Thomas A. Edison*

Date: ——/——/——

"If you don't value your time, neither will others.
Stop giving away your time and talents--start
charging for it." --Kim Garst

Date: ——/——/——

"A successful man is one who can lay a firm foundation with the bricks others have thrown at him." -- David Brinkley

----

Date: ——/——/——

"No one can make you feel inferior without your consent." -- *Eleanor Roosevelt*

Date: ——/——/——

"The whole secret of a successful life is to find out what is one's destiny to do, and then do it." –
–Henry Ford

Date: ——/——/——

"If you're going through hell keep going."

-- Winston Churchill

Date: ——/——/——

"The ones who are crazy enough to think they can change the world, are the ones who do." -- Anonymous

----

Date: ——/——/——

"Don't raise your voice, improve your argument." --Anonymous

Date: ——/——/——

"What seems to us as bitter trials are often blessings in disguise." --Oscar Wilde

----

Date: ____/____/____

"The meaning of life is to find your gift. The purpose of life is to give it away." --Anonymous

----

Date: ——/——/——

"The distance between insanity and genius is measured only by success." --*Bruce Feirstein*

Date: ——/——/——

"When you stop chasing the wrong things, you give the right things a chance to catch you." -- Lolly Daskal

----

Date: ——/——/——

"I believe that the only courage anybody ever needs is the courage to follow your own dreams."
--Oprah Winfrey

Date: ——/——/——

"No masterpiece was ever created by a lazy artist." --Anonymous

----

Date: ——/——/——

"Happiness is a butterfly, which when pursued, is always beyond your grasp, but which, if you will sit down quietly, may alight upon you."

--Nathaniel Hawthorne

Date: ——/——/——

"If you can't explain it simply, you don't understand it well enough." --Albert Einstein

---

Date: ——/——/——

"Life is what happens to you while you're busy making other plans." *John Lennon*

"Eighty percent of success is showing up." Woody Allen

Date: ——/——/——

"Build your own dreams, or someone else will hire you to build theirs." **Farrah Gray**

Date: ——/——/——

"You can't fall if you don't climb. But there's no joy in living your whole life on the ground." Unknown

----

Date: ——/——/——

"Challenges are what make life interesting, and overcoming them is what makes life meaningful." --Joshua Marine

----

Date: ____/____/____

"If you want to lift yourself up, lift up someone else." --Booker T. Washington

---

Date: ——/——/——

"Formal education will make you a living; self-education will make you a fortune." --Jim Rohn

----

Date: ——/——/——

"Your time is limited, so don't waste it living
someone else's life." --Steve Jobs

Date: ——/——/——

"You may be disappointed if you fail, but you are doomed if you don't try." -- Beverly Sills

----

Date: ——/——/——

"Remember, no one can make you feel inferior without your consent." --*Eleanor Roosevelt*

"The question isn't who is going to let me; it's who is going to stop me." --Ayn Rand

----

Date: ——/——/——

"If you do what you've always done, you'll get what you've always gotten." -- Tony Robbins

----

Date: ——/——/——

"Fall seven times and stand up eight." --
Japanese proverb

Date: ——/——/——

"I'm not a product of my circumstances. I'm a product of my decisions." Stephen Covey

----

Date: ——/——/——

"A person who never made a mistake never tried anything new." --Albert Einstein

----

Date: ——/——/——

> "It does not matter how slowly you go as long as you do not stop." -- Confucius